THIS
BLESSÈD
EARTH

BY JOHN HALL WHEELOCK

POETRY
This Blessèd Earth: New and Selected Poems, 1927–1977
By Daylight and In Dream: New and Collected Poems, 1904–1970
Dear Men and Women: New Poems
The Gardener and Other Poems
Poems Old and New
Poems, 1911–1936
The Bright Doom
The Black Panther
Dust and Light
Love and Liberation
The Belovèd Adventure
The Human Fantasy
Verses by Two Undergraduates
   (WITH VAN WYCK BROOKS)

CRITICISM
What Is Poetry?

SELECTED AND EDITED BY
WITH INTRODUCTION
Poets of Today VIII
Poets of Today VII
Poets of Today VI
Poets of Today V
Poets of Today IV
Poets of Today III
Poets of Today II
Poets of Today I
Editor to Author: The Letters of
   Maxwell E. Perkins
The Face of a Nation: Poetical Passages
   from the Writings of Thomas Wolfe

JOHN HALL WHEELOCK

THIS BLESSED EARTH

New and Selected Poems, 1927-1977

CHARLES SCRIBNER'S SONS   NEW YORK

Library of Congress Cataloging in Publication Data
Wheelock, John Hall, 1886–1978
    This blessèd Earth.
    I. Title.
PS3545.H33B54   811'.5'2   78-3844
ISBN 0-684-15727-6

Some of the poems in this volume were first
published in the following publications:
Sewanee Review, Arizona Quarterly, Southern Review,
The New Yorker, Atlantic Monthly,
New York Quarterly, and Bird Effort.

1 3 5 7 9 11 13 15 17 19 V/C 20 18 16 14 12 10 8 6 4 2

Printed in the United States of America

To my friend

JAY B. HUBBELL

in admiration and affection

CONTENTS

9

NEW POEMS

TO YOU, PERHAPS YET UNBORN

It is night, and we are alone together; your head
Bends over the open book, your feeding eyes devour
The substance of my dream. Oh, sacred hour
That makes us one—you, fleeting, and I, already fled!

Here is my joy, here is my sorrow, my heart's rage,
Poured out for you. What tenderness brooding above you
Hallows these poems! I have made them all for you. I love you.
What love, what longing, my reader, speaks to you from this
   page!

SELF-COUNSEL IN AGE

Though much is lost, strange victory has been won,
Exult, my heart, put hope and fear away;
Sing for your own delight—though there be none
To hear you out, sing on while yet you may;
Give thanks for all glad hours beneath the sun;
For peace and eventual liberation pray,
Now the high lonely stars of night come on.

AN ANCIENT STORY

Young thrush, heard singing from some hidden bough
In the west wood nearby,
Your tender song recalls to memory
A day, still unforgotten now,
That blessèd day when we,
My dear true love and I,
After such sundering, such salt seas between,
Once more together, in this same west wood,
Where we so often had together been,
In silence stood,
Listening to your loved song,
Unchanged through all these many years,
And kissed, while the soft May-time green
Swam round us, prismed in our tears.
Oh, if you will,
Sing to us, now as then,
That self-same song—
We are together still,
Bring back again
That day when all was young.

Or, since this may not be—
When, at a not too far-off time, our time is come,
And, under the cloudy shade
Of some, perhaps, young springtime-flowering tree,
Deep in the earth our bodies shall be laid,
Oh, from a hidden bough,
Let fall upon us, where we lie at rest,
Together still, your antique elegy,
The half-remembered story
Of two fond lovers, faithful to their vow,
For love's sake, doubly blest;
Pour out, pour out, upon that quiet air

APHRODITE, 1906

Dark-eyed, out of the snow-cold sea you came,
The young blood under the cheek like dawn-light showing,
Stray tendrils of dark hair in the sea-wind blowing,
Comely and grave, out of the sea you came.

Slim covered thigh and slender stockinged foot
In swift strides over the burnished shingle swinging,
Sweet silence of your smile, soft sea-weed clinging,
Here and there, to the wet bathing-suit.

O fierce and shy, your glance so piercing-true
Shot fire to the struck heart that was as tinder—
The fire of your still loveliness, the tender
High fortitude of the spirit shining through.

And the world was young. O love and song and fame
Were part of youth's still ever believed-in story,
And hope crowned all, when in dear and in queenly glory,
Out of the snow-cold sea to me you came.

REST

Lay your dear head upon
This heart of clay,
We are but dust, now here, now gone,
All things are hastening away—
Here, in this heart of clay,
Love still lives on.
There lay your head.

MELANCHOLIA

There is a place that yet is not a place,
And you have been there. In an empty room,
Walled high and windowless, twin urns of light,
Under the ceiling, cast a somber glow,
And always, somewhere, a lone flute is warbling
Its desultory music. Also always,
From the high shelf along the western wall,
Those effigies look out, of carven stone
Or molded plaster, blessèd artifacts,
Exempt from breathing's harried to-and-fro,
The hounded heart's compulsive laboring—
In bloodless ease at rest, calm, sad, secure,
They wait upon the future, and the eerie
Enchantment of the music lends them there
A strange nobility, a mimic peace,
Such peace as comes after forgotten sorrow,
Dread peace, that follows unremembered joy.

THE CONCERT

After these bleak, these barren days,
Dull bitterness of heart, dull bodily pain,
Beethoven, to hear your voice again,
Your spirit's breath, kindling the orchestra,
Crowding the confluent choiring of the strings
With cries of horn and trumpet, wood-wind clamorings,
Till godhead blazed from every instrument.
Oh, I was lost, I was spent
With blind hunger for this—how did I stray
So far from my heart's country, ever near!
As one released from long imprisonment,
That looks up, suddenly,
To find all starry heaven over him bent,
Or hears, once more, the thunders of the sea,
Beethoven, you set me free:
Myself was given back again to me,
And I came home to the Truth,
Which had been mine—oh, might it ever be—
When, in the marvellous morning of my youth,
I walked this blessèd earth,
Watchful, in adoration and ecstasy.

INTIMATIONS OF MORTALITY

Something that has no existence is absent here
and that absence is louder than any sound.
You have been hearing it all your life
and will hear it
till it grows so faint it overwhelms everything—
as a summer cloud
no bigger than your hand
will blot out the sunset that was never really there.

LIGHT

Dawn-cloud and sunset-cloud catch fire from it.
Whatever it touches, it transfigures.
On whatever it falls, it is like a benediction.
In the depths of the forest, on the innermost leaves,
Patches of gold against jade darkness,
Spilth, drippings of gold
Down tree-trunk and on mossy floor.
Through every cranny and chink the divine elixir runs,
Life-giving, joy-bringing.
Heaven and earth are stained with it,
The effluence of a god.

ADDRESS TO EXISTENCE

While you are still in me
I am enabled to address you,
who, once you have laid me down,
shall be silent indeed—
for, though you have insisted on becoming me,
it is for a limited time only,
and now you are losing interest,
as you always eventually do,
taking up and, in the end, putting down, this one or that one,
be it man or beast, a Michelangelo or an antelope.
Is diversity your purpose, I ask,
or is it that each and every thing must have its chance?
But you are indifferent to my questioning—
we are, at best, your puppets.
Nevertheless, there are moments when I seem to sense
a certain concern, a certain affection even, on your part:
by the way in which you keep my heart beating,
my body's defenses on the alert,
transmuting into my very self the food I eat,
doing for me, every day,
a thousand intricate and marvellous things,
of which I myself am totally incapable,
and so maintaining me as a conscious being.
How can I thank you for this,
for the grand experience of existing,
for remaining me, so many years—
you, who are upstream of language, of thought, of feeling even,
how could there be any way to thank you?
Yet I do thank you. I worship and adore you.
Before you leave me,
before I am no longer able to thank you,
I here do so, with all my heart.
And now lettest thou thy puppet lie down in peace.

AFFIRMATION

We are one self, who are imprisoned here
Upon this turning planet as it swings
Through the lone waste and labyrinth of heaven—
One in our plight, one in our common doom,
One in our stubborn questioning, and one,
Beyond all other creatures, in the sole
Sad consciousness of our predicament—
Pilgrims and outcasts between birth and death,
Scanning the frontiers of the night for news;
Probing the atom; challenging the cell;
Knocking at every gate and every door
Of the inexorable silences;
Wondering; doubting; grieving; worshipping—
Perplexed before the mystery of things.

Now while the earth turns eastward, half in light
And half in darkness; from the Himalayan snows
And Mongol uplands, to the Texan desert
Or where the starry waters dawnward heave
Out of the west from Asia—on blue hills,
'Mid iron cities or green solitudes,
By land or sea, in darkness or in light—
The restless Spirit moves in many ways,
The multitudinous Being is abroad.
We gather in theatres; we brood alone;
We pour with laughter through the shining streets;
We till the earth; we lift our towers to heaven;
We watch beside the sick-bed; on gray capes,
On crags and headlands of the world, we set
Our winking fires, from coast to coast; or wander
The wastes of ocean with a furrowing prow;
We sleep; we turn the pages of a book,
And move, in silence, out of space and time;
We grapple each other; we hate; we fear; we kill;

                                        And us, too
The lonely and inevitable voice
Shall summon, and the silence take us home.
All shall be gathered homeward—he that sang
And he that listened; the lover and the loved,
The lips that pleaded and the hands that blessed,
Lie mingled in the darkness, and these hearts
That beauty haunted be a little dust
Blown round the narrow margins of the world;
We shall be one with the revolving planet
Throughout the ages, till the earth itself,
With all its millions, all its sleeping sons,
Pass, like a cinder, down the Void, or mix
With the primeval fires casting up
The foam of future worlds along the dark.
Perpetual death, perpetual rebirth,
Perpetual passion and perpetual pain!
Is there no respite from the wheel of things?
Is there no refuge from eternity?
The heavens grow old, and hunger for their peace;
The father founts, Antares and Arcturus,
Vega, and Sirius, and the nursling flames—
Ceaselessly dying, ceaselessly reborn—
Tire of the one tune, and find no way
Out of the woven web of space and time,
In which the worlds are tangled; but all move
Through the fierce throes and cycles of rebirth
Laboriously, with groaning forces held
In iron bondage, to the eternal rhythm,
Whose meaning and whose end we may not guess.

What word of courage may I bring to you,
What word of solace or of sustenance?

Our faiths have fallen from us and left us bare;
The dream, fantastic and compassionate,
That like a veil of love and glory hung
Between us and the bitterness of things,
Is lifted, and the universe has grown
Vaster, and much more lonely. Nor shall Thought—
Crying into the dark, and listening, listening—
Get any answer to its prayer: the night
Is soundless and the starry mouths are sealed.

Yet the deep heart still knows that all is well
And the truth greater than we dare to dream,
Greater and more exalted! Though the mind,
Fashioned for humbler uses, may not grasp
The meaning of the mystery; though Thought—
For all its longing, all its labor—gain
Hardly the comfort of a hope, there is
A self within us, wiser than the mind,
And deeper than all thought, that still endures
Firm at the helm through all the storms of chance
Forever, in unquenchable belief
And courage not to be abated: life,
In rage and fear, in love and agony,
Weaving her splendor from the dust of death,
Bears in her breast—though inarticulate—
A holier confidence; her running grass,
Her herds trampling the uplands, her fierce wills
In bush and brake, her ravening hosts that throng
The fields of ocean and the aisles of air—
Furious, furious, for continuance—
These answer, these bear witness, all is well;
These in indomitable zest affirm
The wonder and glory of a universe

In which all lusts, all hungers, all defeats,
All agonies, are woven to one Doom,
And every heart-beat is an act of faith
Praising the hidden purpose!

                         Stern, indeed,
Are the realities; the wheel of heaven
Revolves, with all its motions, and the planet
Heaves forward blindly, bearing us along
Into the Void—we know not why nor where;
Embattled between two oblivions
We stand, for a brief moment, and lift up
Our faces to the light—but in our blood
The voices of the generations past
Strive, and the generations yet unborn
Are urgent in us that we play our part,
As actors in a stately tragedy,
To some triumphant close. Courage and faith,
These will best serve us here. And as for Him
Whom we have sought beyond the stars in vain,
Perhaps He may be nearer than we know.

MIDNIGHT CONTEMPLATION

I have looked upon you, O Truth,
O infinite stream of the stars—
I have seen you, O Very Truth.
Now let me take my rest.

O infinite stream of the stars,
Whose glory once trembled in me,
Bend over me while I sleep.

THE HOLY EARTH

In the immense cathedral of the holy earth,
Whose arches are the heavens and the great vault above
Groined with its myriad stars, what miracles of birth,
What sacraments of death, what rituals of love!

Her nave is the wide world and the whole length of it,
One flame on all her altars kindles her many fires;
Wherever the clear tapers of trembling life are lit
Resound for joy the old, indomitable choirs.

The holy church of earth with clamorous worshippers
Is crowded, and fierce hungers, faithful every one
To the one faith; that stern and simple faith of hers
Contents the heart that asks no pity, giving none.

Each on the other feeds, and all on each are fed,
And each for all is offered—a living offering, where
In agony and triumph the ancient feast is spread,
Life's sacramental supper, that all her sons may share.

They mingle with one another, blend—mingle—merge,
    and flow
Body into wild body; in rapture endlessly
Weaving, with intricate motions of being, to and fro,
The pattern of all Being, one mighty harmony:

One Body, of all bodies woven and interwrought—
One Self, in many selves, through their communion
In love and death, made perfect, wherein each self is
    nought
Save as it serve the many, mysteriously made One.

And all are glad for life's sake, and all have found it
     good
From the beginning; all, through many and warring ways,
In savage vigor of life and wanton hardihood
Live out, like a brave song, the passion of their days.

With music woven of lust and music woven of pain,
Chapel and aisle and choir, the great cathedral rings—
One voice in all her voices chanting the old disdain
Of pity, the clean hunger of all primal things.

From the trembling of Arcturus even to the tiny nest
Of the grey mouse, the glories of her vast frame extend:
The span of her great arches, stretching from east to west,
Is measureless—the immense reaches are without end.

                    *   *   *

Evening closes. The light from heaven's west window falls
Graver and softer now. In vain the twilight pleads
With stubborn night—his shadow looms on the massive
     walls.
Darkness. The immemorial ritual proceeds.

The spider in her quivering web watches and waits;
The moth flutters entangled, in agony of fear
He beats among the toils that bind him; she hesitates
Along the trembling wires—she pauses—she draws near,

She weaves her delicate bondage around him; in the net,
As in a shroud, he labors—but, labor as he will,
The cunning threads hold fast; her drowsy mouth is set
Against the body that shivers softly, and is still.

And through the leafy dark the owl with noiseless flight
Moves, peering craftily among the tangled trees
And thickets of the wood all slumbrous in the night—
The fledgling's bitter cry comes sharp upon the breeze.

With dreadful ceremony all things together move
To the one end: shrill voices in triumph all around
Prolong deliriously their monotone of love—
Arches and aisles are heavy with incense and dim sound.

Hush, the whole world is kneeling! Murmurous is the
        air—
The Host is lifted up. Upon the altar lies
The sacramental Body. The wind breathes like a prayer—
Solemnly is renewed the eternal sacrifice.

With mingled moan and might of warring wills made one
The vast cathedral shudders. From chancel, nave and
        choir
Sounds the fierce hymn to life: her holy will be done!
Upon her myriad altars flames the one sacred fire.

THE BLACK PANTHER

There is a panther caged within my breast,
But what his name, there is no breast shall know
Save mine, nor what it is that drives him so,
Backward and forward, in relentless quest—
That silent rage, baffled but unsuppressed,
The soft pad of the stealthy feet that go
Over my body's prison to and fro,
Trying the walls forever without rest.

All day I feed him with my living heart,
But when the night puts forth her dreams and stars,
The inexorable frenzy reawakes:
His wrath is hurled upon the trembling bars,
The eternal passion stretches me apart,
And I lie silent—but my body shakes.

BONAC

Du bist Orplid, mein Land, das ferne leuchtet—MÖRIKE

1

This is enchanted country, lies under a spell,
Bird-haunted, ocean-haunted—land of youth,
Land of first love, land of death also, perhaps,
And desired return. Sea-tang and honeysuckle
Perfume the air, where the old house looks out
Across mild lowlands, meadows of scrub and pine,
A shell echoing the sea's monotone
That haunts these shores. And here, all summer through,
From dawn to dusk, there will be other music,
Threading the sea's music: at rise of sun,
With jubilation half-awakened birds
Salute his coming again, the lord of life,
His ambulatory footstep over the earth,
Who draws after him all that tide of song—
Salute the oncoming day, while from the edges
Of darkness, westward, fading voices call,
Night's superseded voices, the whip-poor-will's
Lamentation and farewell. Morning and noon
And afternoon and evening, the singing of birds
Lies on this country like an incantation:
Robin and wren, catbird, phoebe and chat,
Song-sparrow's music-box tune, and from the slender
Arches of inmost shade, the woodland's roof,
Where few winds come, flutelike adagio or
Wild syrinx-cry and high raving of the thrush,
Their clang and piercing pierce the spirit through—
Look off into blue heaven, you shall witness
Angelic motions, the volt and sidewise shift
Of the swallow in mid-air. Enchanted land,
Where time has died; old ocean-haunted land;

Land of first love, where grape and honeysuckle
Tangle their vines, where the beach-plum in spring
Snows all the inland dunes; bird-haunted land,
Where youth still dwells forever, your long day
Draws to its close, bringing for evening-star
Venus, a bud of fire in the pale west,
Bringing dusk and the whip-poor-will again,
And the owl's tremolo and the firefly,
And gradual darkness. Silently the bat,
Over still lawns that listen to the sea,
Weaves the preoccupation of his flight.
The arch of heaven soars upward with all its stars.

2

Summer fades soon here, autumn in this country
Comes early and exalted. Where the wild land,
With its sparse bayberry and huckleberry,
Slopes seaward, where the seaward dunes go down,
Echoing, to the sea; over the beaches,
Over the shore-line stretching east and west,
The ineffable slant light of autumn lingers.
The roof of heaven is higher now, the clouds
That drag, trailing, along the enormous vault,
Hang higher, the wide ways are wider now.
Sea-hawks wander the ocean solitudes,
Sea-winds walk there, the waters grow turbulent,
And inland also a new restlessness
Walks the world, remembering something lost,
Seeking something remembered: wheeling wings
And songless woods herald the great departure,
Cattle stray, swallows gather in flocks,

The cloud-travelling moon through gusty cloud
Looks down on the first pilgrims going over,
And hungers in the blood are whispering, "Flee!
Seek otherwhere, here is no lasting home."
Now bird-song fails us, now an older music
Is vibrant in the land—the drowsy cry
Of grasshopper and cricket, earth's low cry
Of sleepy love, her inarticulate cry,
Calling life downward, promising release
From these vague longings, these immortal torments.
The drowsy voice drones on—oh, siren voice:
Aeons of night, millenniums of repose,
Soundless oblivion, divine surcease,
Dark intermingling with the primal darkness,
Oh, not to be, to slough this separate being,
Flow home at last! The alert spirit listens,
Hearing, meanwhile, far off, along the coast,
Rumors of the rhythm of some wakeful thing,
Reverberations, oceanic tremors,
The multitudinous motions of the sea,
With all its waters, all its warring waves.

THE FISH-HAWK

On the large highway of the ample air that flows
Unbounded between sea and heaven, while twilight
    screened
The sorrowful distances, he moved and had repose;
On the huge wind of the immensity he leaned
His steady body, in long lapse of flight—and rose

Gradual, through broad gyres of ever-climbing rest,
Up the clear stair of the untrammelled sky, and stood
Throned on the summit! Slowly, with his widening breast,
Widened around him the enormous solitude,
From the gray rim of ocean to the glowing west.

Headlands and capes forlorn, of the far coast, the land
Rolling her barrens toward the west, he, from his throne
Upon the gigantic wind, beheld: he hung, he fanned
The abyss, for mighty joy, to feel beneath him strown
Pale pastures of the sea, with heaven on either hand—

The world, with all her winds and waters, earth and air,
Fields, folds, and moving clouds. The awful and adored
Arches and endless aisles of vacancy, the fair
Void of sheer heights and hollows, hailed him as her lord
And lover in the highest, to whom all heaven lay bare.

Till from that tower of ecstasy, that baffled height,
Stooping, he sank; and slowly on the world's wide way
Walked, with great wing on wing, the merciless, proud
    Might,
Hunting the huddled and lone reaches for his prey,
Down the dim shore—and faded in the crumbling light.

Slowly the dusk covered the land. Like a great hymn
The sound of moving winds and waters was; the sea
Whispered a benediction, and the west grew dim
Where evening lifted her clear candles quietly. . . .
Heaven, crowded with stars, trembled from rim to rim.

THE DIVINE INSECT

Already it's late summer. Sun-bathers go
Earlier now. Except for those who lie
Dazed between sea-music and radio
The beach is bare as the blue bowl of the sky,
Where a cloud floats, solitary and slow.

And up the beach, where at mid-summer's height
One gull with occasional lurch and pause would steer
Onward his leisurely loose-winged casual flight,
Gull wings weave patterns, their noise floods the ear
Like a fugue, cry answering cry in hoarse delight.

Now on the beach there also may be found,
Straddled in mimic flight, with arching wing
Spread either way, some gull swift death has downed
There, like a tumbled kite whose severed string
Kept it in heaven by binding it to the ground.

Inland, when the slant evening sun-beams touch
Leaves, long obscured in tunnelled shade, to flame,
The divine insect, for I called him such,
Begins his high thin music. To my shame
I never learned what he was, who owe him so much.

Listening to his frail song, so pure, so dim,
I made my poems, he was mystery's decoy,
Something far and lost, just over the rim
Of being, or so I felt, and as a boy
I wove fantastic notions about him.

Throughout long evenings and hushed midnights when
Grasshoppers shrilled, his barely perceptible note
Wound on like a thread of time, while my pen
Made its own scratchy music as I wrote.
The divine insect and I were comrades then.

That high hypnotic note opened some door
On a world seemingly come upon by chance,
But a world, surely, I had known before.
Deeper I sank into a timeless trance—
Strange thoughts and fancies troubled me more and more.

I could pass through that minuscule sound, it seemed to me,
As through a fine tube, getting smaller and still more small,
Until I was smaller than nothing—then, suddenly,
Come to the other end of the tube, and crawl
Out, into glittering immensity.

For, if by travelling west you shall come east
Or, as Einstein has it, the continuum
Curves on itself, may we not through the least
Come to the largest, and so finally come
Back where we were, undiminished and unincreased?

Since then, I have tried to put this into verse,
But language limits the sense it often mars—
I still believe, for better or for worse,
We look through one atom into all the stars,
In the note of one insect hear the universe.

These few green acres where so many a day
Has found me, acres I have loved so long,
Have the whole galaxy for crown, and stay
Unspoiled by that. Here in some thrush's song
I have heard things that took my breath away.

It is a country out of the world's ken,
Time has no power upon it. Year on year,
Summer unfolds her pageant here again—
I have looked deep into all being here
Through one loved place far from the storms of men.

Here often, day and night, there will be heard
The sea's grave rhythm, a dark undertone
Beneath the song of insect or of bird—
Sea-voices by sea-breezes landward blown,
And shudder of leaves by the soft sea-wind stirred.

In the jade light and gloom of woodland walks
The spider lily and slender shinleaf stand,
The catbird from his treetop pulpit talks
The morning up, and in the meadowland
The velvet mullein lift their woolly stalks.

The world grows old. Ageless and undefiled
These stay, meadow and thicket, wood and hill:
The green fly wears her golden dress, the wild
Grape is in bloom, the fork-tailed swallow still
Veers on the wind as when I was a child.

And in mid-August, when the sun has set
And the first star out of the west shows through,
The divine insect, as I call him yet,
Begins his high thin note, so pure, so true,
Putting me ever deeper in his debt.

The old enchantment takes me as before,
I listen, half in dream, hearing by chance
The soft lapse of the sea along the shore,
And sink again into that timeless trance,
Deeper and deeper now, and more and more.

WOOD-THRUSH

Behind the wild-bird's throat
An Eden, more remote
Than Adam knew of, lies—
The primal paradise
Lost, yet forever here.
From that wild syrinx cries
Into the listening ear,
The labyrinthine heart,
A longing, a regret,
In which it has no part.
Where the young leaves are met
In overarching green
Soft winds stir and divide,
Where shadows cloud and throng
The coverts in between,
That early bud of song
Opens its petals wide,
Becomes a three-fold star
Of voices twined and blent,
Happy and innocent,
Within whose singing are
Troy lost and Hector slain,
Judas and Golgotha,
The longing and the pain,
Sorrows of old that were
And joy come back again
From ages earlier,
Before joy's course was run,
Before time's bounds were set—
The fountains of the sun
Are in that twining jet
Of song, so clear, so cool.
While the false heart raves on,

All these you loved and left. We may not stay
Long with the joy our hearts are set upon:
This is a thing that here you tried to say.

The night has fallen; the day's work is done;
Your groves, your lawns, the passion of this place,
Cry out your love of them—but you are gone.

O father, whom I may no more embrace
In childish fervor, but, standing far apart,
Look on your spirit rather than your face,

Time now has touched me also, and my heart
Has learned a sadness that yours earlier knew,
Who labored here, though with the greater art.

The truth is on me now that was with you:
How life is sweet, even its very pain,
The years how fleeting and the days how few.

Truly, your labors have not been in vain;
These woods, these walks, these gardens—everywhere
I look, the glories of your love remain.

Therefore, for you, now beyond praise or prayer,
Before the night falls that shall make us one,
In which neither of us will know or care,

This kiss, father, from him who was your son.

HERRING-GULL

Run seaward, launch upon the air, and sound your desolate
    cry
Over these shores and waters; the wind on which you
    rest
Air-borne, as sea-borne on the ocean's undulant breast,
Buoys you on, hunting the waste with hungry eye.

Are there, beyond these crowded shores, beyond your call
And waiting your return to their sandy bed,
Young, ravenous beaks strained skyward, gaping to be
    fed?
A need is on you, a great need is on us all.

Balance upon the wind, send out your desolate cry
To the four corners of the waste, your clamor is
The clamor of life in bondage to the old necessities—
Torment that is the thrust of some immortal joy.

NIGHT THOUGHTS IN AGE

Light, that out of the west looked back once more
Through lids of cloud, has closed a sleepy eye;
The heaven of stars bends over me its silence,
A harp through which the wind of time still whispers
Music some hand has hushed but left there trembling—
Conceits of an aging man who lies awake
Under familiar rafters, in this leafy
Bird-singing, haunted, green, ancestral spot
Where time has made such music! For often now,
In this belovèd country whose coastal shores
Look seaward, without limit, to the south—
Land of flung spume and spray, sea-winds and -voices
Where the gull rides the gale on equal wing,
With motionless body and forward-looking head,
Where, in mid-summer days, offshore, the dolphin
Hurdles the water with arching leap and plunge—
I meditate, lying awake, alone,
On the sea's voice and time's receding music,
Felt ebbing in the heart and shrunken vein—
How time, that takes us all, will at the last,
In taking us, take the whole world we are dreaming:
Sun, wind and sea, whisper of rain at night,
The young, hollow-cheeked moon, the clouds of evening
Drifting in a great solitude—all these
Shall time take away, surely, and the face
From which the eyes of love look out at us
In this brief world, this horror-haunted kingdom
Of beauty and of longing and of terror,
Of phantoms and illusion, of appearance
And disappearance—magic of leger-de-main,
Trick of the prestidigitator's wand—
The huge phantasmagoria we are dreaming:
This shall time take from us, and take forever,
When we are taken by that receding music.
O marvel of things, fabulous dream, too soon,

Too soon will the wild blood cry out and death
Quell, with one blow, the inscrutable fantasy!
Shall prayer change this? Youth is the hour for prayer,
That has so much to pray for; a man's life,
Lived howsoever, is a long reconcilement
To the high, lonely, unforgiving truth,
Which will not change for his or any prayer,
Now or hereafter: in that reconcilement
Lies all of wisdom. Age is the hour for praise,
Praise that is joy, praise that is acquiescence
Praise that is adoration and gratitude
For all that has been given and not been given.
Night flows on. The wind, that all night through
Quickened the treetops with a breath of ocean,
Veers inland, falls away, and the sea's voice,
Learned in lost childhood, a remembered music,
By day or night, through love, through sleep, through dream,
Still breathing its perpetual benediction,
Has dwindled to a sigh. By the west window,
In the soft dark the leaves of the sycamore
Stir gently, rustle, and are still, are listening
To a silence that is music. The old house
Is full of ghosts, dear ghosts on stair and landing,
Ghosts in chamber and hall; garden and walk
Are marvellous with ghosts, where so much love
Dwelt for a little while and made such music,
Before it too was taken by the tide
That takes us all, of time's receding music.
Oh, all is music! All has been turned to music!
All that is vanished has been turned to music!
And these familiar rafters, that have known
The child, the young man and the man, now shelter
The aging man, who lies here, listening, listening—
All night, in a half dream, I have lain here listening.

DARK JOY

1

What dark Force, striving for more tendrils, more surfaces,
Has multiplied Itself in us as a tree is multiplied in its
    leaves?
The sleeping One awakens into the many.
We are fragments of a broken Thing,
To be conscious is to be separate.
This is the dark joy of being,
This is the tragedy at the root of being,
For separation brings with it death.
With pain and with death we pay for our separateness.
The Undying is born and dies in Its mortal members.
The great Unity is broken, and self is arrayed against self.
From this all torments flow.
Therefore Jesus preached love, which, in some measure,
    bridges that separation,
And unselfishness, which tempers the fury of the struggle.
Therefore the Buddha preached the need to escape from
    life and death.
Yet all is exchange. Nothing is lost from these siftings.

2

Exult, and have joy in this day's sun, all living things!
Take delight in his presence today, for it was he who drew
    you forth.
In his presence, you are in the presence of your visible
    creator.
The Power behind him you are not permitted to behold.
As he is the visible father, the earth is your mother,
And the sea your foster-mother.
With her, still dwell your younger brothers and sisters,

Who also were fathered of the sun, though they may not
    look up to him.

3

Exult, all living things, in this life, this moment!
You will not be again, but others shall be, and you will be
    those others.
Though life perish from the planet, the planet will give birth
    to it once more.
Though the planet be destroyed, new planets shall be created
    and will renew it.

4

Exult, all creatures everywhere, for pain is better than
    nothingness, and joy is still better.
Exult with the dark joy of being.
Exult, all you whales of the sea!
Exult, all you little foxes that have your dens in the earth!
Exult, you dwellers on distant galaxies!
For to live and to die is good.
So say the crickets and cicadas, all night long, outside my
    window here.
So says the oriole who wakes me each morning from the elm
    that arches the old house.
So say the ailanthus trees stretching toward it their green
    fronds with leaves on either side as many as the feet
    of the caterpillar, and every leaf held out to receive the
    light.

SONG ON REACHING SEVENTY

Shall not a man sing as the night comes on?
He would be braver than the bird
That shrieks for terror, and is gone
Into the gathering dark; and he has heard
Often, at evening's hush,
Upon some towering sunset bough
A belated thrush
Lift up his heart against the menacing night,
Till silence covered all. Oh, now
Before the coming of a greater night,
How bitterly sweet and dear
All things have grown! How shall we bear the brunt,
The fury and joy of every sound and sight,
Now almost cruelly fierce with all delight:
The clouds of dawn that blunt
The spearhead of the sun; the clouds that stand,
Raging with light, around his burial;
The rain-pocked pool
At the wood's edge; a bat's skittering flight
Over the sunset-colored land;
Or, heard toward morning, the cock pheasant's call!
Oh, every sight and sound
Has meaning now! Now, also, love has laid
Upon us her old chains of tenderness,
So that to think of the belovèd one,
Love is so great, is to be half afraid—
It is like looking at the sun,
That blinds the eye with truth.
Yet longing remains unstilled,
Age will look into the face of youth
With longing, over a gulf not to be crossed.
Oh, joy that is almost pain, pain that is joy,
Unimaginable to the younger man or boy—

Nothing is quite fulfilled,
Nothing is lost;
But all is multiplied, till the heart almost
Aches with its burden: there and here
Become as one, the present and the past;
The dead, who were content to lie
Far from us, have consented to draw near—
We are thronged with memories,
Move amid two societies,
And learn at last
The dead are the only ones who never die.

Great night, hold back
A little longer yet your mountainous, black
Waters of darkness from this shore,
This island garden, this paradisal spot,
The haunt of love and pain,
Which we must leave, whether we would or not,
And where we shall not come again.
More time—oh, but a little more,
Till, stretched to the limits of being, the taut heart break,
Bursting the bonds of breath,
Shattering the wall
Between us and our world, and we awake
Out of the dream of self into the truth of all,
The price for which is death.

UNISON

There is a secret that the sober mood
Of science misses, it will not be bought
By the contriving mind however shrewd—

Within the cell, within the atom sought,
Within the inner center's whirling rings,
Sits the demonic joy that laughs at thought

And is the face behind the mask of things,
And is the measure of the choric dance,
The music of the song Creation sings.

Who shall unweave the web of Circumstance,
Or trace the pattern in the fugitive
And shifting tapestry of change and chance?

Or, having learned the pattern, who shall give
The answer then? What answer has been given
Ever, to any man, why man should live!

Not in the flesh, not in the spirit even,
Not in the cunning of the brain that rides
In mastery upon the roads of heaven,

Or charts the rhythm of the starry tides,
The answer and the truth are found, but where,
Deep at the very core, the Stranger bides—

And pours his courage through the heart's despair,
And works his healing in the body's wound,
And sheds his glory through the spirit. There

The answer is, the wisdom shall be found,
Which is the answer of the greening tree,
Which is the wisdom of the fruitful ground—

A wisdom older and more wise than we,
Dumb with a secret difficult to tell,
And inarticulate with mystery,

For, to define it, were a miracle.
Oh, not in the low moments but the great
The exultant rhythm is made audible

That sways the music at the heart of Fate,
To which Time in his passage and return
Moves, and the burdened systems, with their weight

Of suns and planets, revolving as they burn—
The harmony in which all modes are bent
To the one meaning that they all must learn,

Of many and divergent meanings blent,
Of motions intricate and manifold,
With various voices weaving one consent!

Nor is it easy for the mind to hold
The extreme joy of things, or bear for long
The exalted beauty, hidden from of old,

Whose sure intent, immutable and strong,
Secret and tireless and undeterred,
Moves through the mazes of the winding song—

And whosoever in his heart has heard
That music, all his life shall toil to say
The passion of it. But there is no word—

No words are made for it. There is no way.

EVENING CONTEMPLATION

Over the meadow-land
Where I so often have watched them,
To an ancient sound of the sea
Heavy upon this coast,
The summer stars look down—
A part of them, yet separate,
Singled by consciousness,
I stand and survey them here.
Deneb, Vega, Altair,
Hang high in the pure vault,
Trembling, and far below them
Venus, a fiery bloom
Fallen from the bough of heaven,
The great galactic vine,
Is glowing deep in the west.
Now from the fields unnumbered
Small creatures lift their hymn,
Cricket and grasshopper
Welcome with shrill noise
The illustrious presences,
They are here, they are here, they are here,
The glory that dwells in darkness
Has visited earth once more.
The heavens preserve their secret,
From the rim of the huge vault
To the high sidereal arches
No sound. Perpetual silence!
Infinite peace! But oh,
Universe of hushed light,
That peace will not deceive me;
Horrible process, divine
Agony and splendor,
Too well I know your ways,

Their grandeur and their vileness:
The tenderness, the brute
Bestiality, the bloody
Pattern of things on earth,
The fangs that rend the living
Body, the cruel delight,
The terror and the torment,
I know them—and in the heavens
Your dread and violent way
From nebula to system,
The throes of your vast elation,
Convulsions, whirlwinds of stars,
Fierce galaxies without number,
Staining the virgin darkness.
Also, the high sublime
Way of your lonely dreaming
In arches of ordered color
Where the rainbow curves the light
Over a trailing cloud,
The sorrow of void sea-spaces,
And the bolt of bright flame,
And the listening heart of a mother—
I know them, O divine truth,
Who stand here, for a moment
Permitted while the red blood
In leaping faithfulness flushes
Body and brain with the old
Incomparable elixir—
Permitted so, for a time,
To be aware of you now,
To worship and to adore you,
Holy substance of things,
From which the body of love

Is fashioned, the oceanic
Rhythm, the wild spring rain,
And the music of a Beethoven,
And of which I too am part
Forever. Oh, consoling
Thought, forever, forever
One with your timeless being,
More fully even than now,
When the temporal separation
Through consciousness shall be ended,
That consciousness in which
So briefly you were mirrored;
O sole and perfect truth,
When I lie down to mix
With your beauty in the darkness,
When I drag your glory down,
With me, into the grave.

DEAR MEN AND WOMEN

(In memory of Van Wyck Brooks)

In the quiet before cockcrow when the cricket's
Mandolin falters, when the light of the past
Falling from the high stars yet haunts the earth
And the east quickens, I think of those I love—
Dear men and women no longer with us.

And not in grief or regret merely but rather
With a love that is almost joy I think of them,
Of whom I am part, as they of me, and through whom
I am made more wholly one with the pain and the glory,
The heartbreak at the heart of things.

I have learned it from them at last, who am now grown old
A happy man, that the nature of things is tragic
And meaningful beyond words, that to have lived
Even if once only, once and no more,
Will have been—oh, how truly—worth it.

The years go by: March flows into April,
The sycamore's delicate tracery puts on
Its tender green; April is August soon;
Autumn, and the raving of insect choirs,
The thud of apples in moonlit orchards;

Till winter brings the slant, windy light again
On shining Manhattan, her towering stone and glass;
And age deepens—oh, much is taken, but one
Dearer than all remains, and life is sweet
Still, to the now enlightened spirit.

Doors are opened that never before were opened,
New ways stand open, but quietly one door
Closes, the door to the future; there it is written,
"Thus far and no farther"—there, as at Eden's gate,
The angel with the fiery sword.

The Eden we dream of, the Eden that lies before us,
The unattainable dream, soon lies behind.
Eden is always yesterday or tomorrow,
There is no way now but back, back to the past—
The past has become paradise.

And there they dwell, those ineffable presences,
Safe beyond time, rescued from death and change.
Though all be taken, they only shall not be taken—
Immortal, unaging, unaltered, faithful yet
To that lost dream world they inhabit.

Truly, to me they now may come no more,
But I to them in reverie and remembrance
Still may return, in me they still live on;
In me they shall have their being, till we together
Darken in the great memory.

Dear eyes of delight, dear youthful tresses, foreheads
Furrowed with age, dear hands of love and care—
Lying awake at dawn, I remember them,
With a love that is almost joy I remember them:
Lost, and all mine, all mine, forever.